USELESS FACTS
about → DACHSHUNDS

OVERVIEW

OVERVIEW

OVERVIEW

CHAPTER 1

Dachshund origin
From hunting hero to couch potato

Dachshund origin
From hunting hero to couch potato

1 The dachshund was originally bred in Germany to drive badgers out of their burrows. Its name comes from the German word "Dachs." Today, it has traded the forests for sofas, transforming from a brave hunting dog into the king of the couch.

2 Its long body and short legs made the dachshund perfect for underground hunting. But while it once explored badger sets, it now prefers warm blankets and cozy spots—the life of a couch potato is simply more appealing.

3 Dachshunds were bred for hunting in different sizes to suit different animals. From the standard dachshund to the miniature dachshund, they were true hunting experts. Today, size only matters when it comes to cuddling.

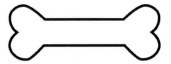

4 In the Middle Ages, dachshunds were considered heroes underground. They fought badgers and other animals. Today, they only fight against vacuum cleaners and their master's rules when they think they don't make sense.

5 The breed became known for its tenacity and courage, even when facing larger animals. These qualities make them truly outstanding personalities to this day— both on the hunt and in everyday life with their owners.

6 In the 19th century, dachshunds were a symbol of strength and courage. Today, they symbolize humor and friendliness— but they have never lost their strong character. A true dachshund always retains a personality.

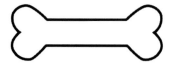

Dachshund origin
From hunting hero to couch potato

7 The Dachshund's coat types—short-haired, long-haired, and wire-haired—originated to adapt to different environments and hunting styles. Today, they are more fashionable variations that make the Dachshund even more versatile.

8 Dachshunds were bred to work independently and make decisions—traits they retain to this day. This independence is especially evident when deciding when it's time for treats.

9 The popularity of the Dachshund soon led to its appreciation beyond the hunting scene. Its charm and unique appearance made it a favorite in households around the world—and not just among hunters.

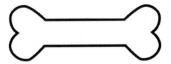

10 The dachshund became so popular that it soon began appearing in works of art and literature. Its character and appearance inspired many artists. Today, it is a social media star, bringing smiles to people around the world.

11 During World War I, the dachshund became unpopular in the United States because of its association with Germany. However, its charm quickly overcame this setback, and today it is one of the most popular dog breeds in the world.

12 The dachshund's hunting technique was unique: courageous, precise, and persistent. These qualities are still evident today when it picks up a scent—be it a squirrel or the scent of a lost snack.

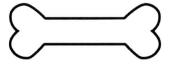

Dachshund origin
From hunting hero to couch potato

13 In the past, a dachshund had no fear of large animals. Badgers and wild boars were his enemies. Today, he displays the same courage - be it against vacuum cleaners, squirrels, or other "dangers" of his modern kingdom.

14 Dachshunds were originally kept in packs for more efficient hunting. But they also proved themselves as solitary animals. Today, they are pack animals within their own family and are not afraid to take the lead.

15 In the past, the dachshund fought badgers twice his size. Today, he fights against blankets that aren't perfectly arranged. His motto hasn't changed: "Never give up, even if the opponents are fluffy or heavy!"

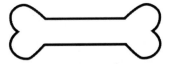

CHAPTER 2

Dachshund records
Short legs, big ego

16 The world's longest dachshund was "Otto," a mix who measured an impressive 2.10 meters with tail and snout. Although he looked more like a stretch limo, he remained true to his sausage image. A true champion of length who belongs in every Guinness Book of Records.

17 A dachshund named "Chanel" from the USA holds the record for the world's oldest dog. She lived to an impressive age of 21 years and 114 days. Her secret? A lot of love, a little luck, and probably the stubbornness to stay longer because she hadn't experienced enough yet.

18 In 2013, the California dachshund "Twinkie" burst into the record books. He popped 100 balloons in just 60 seconds. His paw dexterity was impressive, his enthusiasm unmistakable. A true master of balloon hunting!

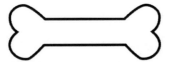

Dachshund records
Short legs, big ego

19 The longest ears of a dachshund reached an impressive 32 centimeters. The owner had to hold them while running to prevent his dog from tripping over them. A record that shows that sometimes even a dachshund can have too much of a good thing.

20 At the "Wiener Dog Race" in the USA, hundreds of dachshunds meet every year to test their speed. Whether they win or lose, the real star is always their little belly, which barely leaves the ground while running. A spectacle guaranteed to make you laugh.

21 Dachshund "Rocky" from Great Britain set the record for the loudest bark: At an incredible 115 decibels, he was as loud as a chainsaw. Rocky was probably accidentally woken up by the bell – neighbors still remember it today.

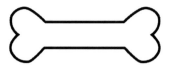

14

Dachshund records
Short legs, big ego

22 "Shorty," a Viennese dachshund, won the title of fastest-eating dachshund in 2020. He devoured 20 mini sausages in just 60 seconds. No one knows how he managed it, but Shorty seemed still hungry after the record-breaking chase.

23 In the world's largest dachshund parade, 3,000 dachshunds gathered in Krakow. An army of small legs and big personalities filled every street. It was the longest dachshund walk in history—and everyone loved it.

24 A dachshund from Texas set a high jump record. Despite his short legs, he managed to leap over a meter. Proof that there's only one limit to dachshunds: When it comes to food, they'll do anything.

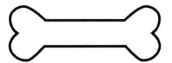

25 Dachshund "Max" accidentally ran a full marathon. He actually just wanted to find his owner, but he persisted and finished the course. A record for little paws, proving that endurance isn't always a matter of leg length.

26 "Peanut," the dachshund from California, won the title for best costume. In 2019, he appeared at a Halloween show dressed as a hot dog—complete with bun. Pure irony, but everyone who saw him had to laugh. And Peanut apparently thought it was pretty cool.

27 The fastest stair climber among the dachshunds managed 30 steps in just 10 seconds. What sounds like a sports record was probably more of an escape from the vacuum cleaner. Dachshunds know their priorities.

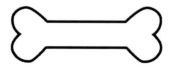

28 "Muffin," a US dachshund, balanced seven treats on his nose – maintaining the calm of a Zen master. They were only devoured on command. A true record of patience, probably motivated only by the subsequent feast.

29 The dachshund "Fritz" shoveled ten meters of snow in just five minutes. It was probably just a lot of fun for him. It's a miracle to us that his short legs can even function as a snowplow.

30 The "Wiener Dog" from the USA set a patience record: He sat motionless in front of a sausage for 15 minutes. Absolute torture for a dachshund, but also proof that these little dogs continue to break records.

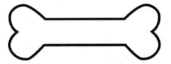

CHAPTER 3

Dachshund biology
How much sausage fits in?

31 The dachshund has 50 different muscles in its tail that work together perfectly. Wagging it shows joy, staying still shows excitement, and a slight tremor signals, "Where's my food? I clearly haven't eaten enough."

32 A dachshund's heart beats about 60–100 times per minute. However, as soon as a food bowl is filled or a squirrel is spotted, it accelerates rapidly—which explains why excitement in dachshunds is almost always snack- or hunting-related.

33 A dachshund's nose is a superpower: With around 220 million olfactory cells, it's 40 times more powerful than a human's. A lost treat or a crumb under the sofa? A dachshund will reliably find it, often faster than you can blink.

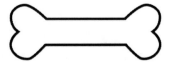

Dachshund biology
How much sausage fits in?

34 Dachshund eyes not only detect movement better, but also seem to always know exactly what you're hiding. Their loyal gaze seems cute, but it's a tactical masterpiece for luring snacks out of your hand.

35 A dachshund can easily eat 20% of its own weight in food. Its stomach expands considerably, making it a true "second helping expert." However, it will never convince you that it's already had enough.

36 The dachshund's long ears serve an important function: As it sniffs, they sweep the air directly to its nose, helping it perceive scents even more intensely. A perfect design—and a relentless search for food trails.

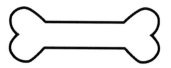

37 Dachshunds are true digging experts. Their strong front paws have large claws, ideal for digging. Originally used to hunt badgers, today this means that no garden is safe from an enthusiastic dachshund.

38 The dachshund has a long digestive tract relative to its size. What goes in must come out quickly—an efficient system that fills the bowl more often and necessitates more frequent walks. A true cycle of dachshund happiness.

39 The dachshund's short legs stem from a genetic condition called chondrodysplasia. It sounds complicated, but it's what makes the breed so charming: low ground clearance, but plenty of courage and character.

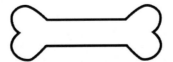

40 A dachshund can locate sounds from different directions by moving its ears independently of each other. This way, it never misses a sound—be it the refrigerator door or a treat dropped unnoticed on the floor.

41 Dachshund paws are particularly strong, allowing them to dig deep. Their toes are broad and well-padded, which helps them find their footing even on uneven terrain. A carpet or sandbox? A true playground for a dachshund.

42 A dachshund can hear sounds up to four times better than humans. They can hear the sound of a bag of chips you open through closed doors and multiple walls. Secret snacking? Forget it; the dachshund always wins.

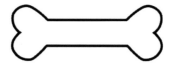

43 Dachshunds have an amazing auditory memory. Hear the sound of a treat just once, and they'll never forget it. In the future, you'll not only recognize the sound, but your dachshund will also remind you of it.

44 A dachshund's nose can distinguish between smells that are several days old. This explains why he can even find a cookie that slipped unnoticed under the cupboard a week ago.

45 The dachshund has a lung capacity that allows it to bark extremely long and loudly. Originally an advantage during hunting, today it's more of a reminder that the postman has been at the gate again without permission.

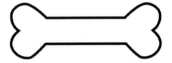

CHAPTER 4

Dackel-Stories
Adventure in miniature

46 A dachshund from Bavaria once ran 10 kilometers behind a train because his owner had boarded. At the destination station, passengers greeted him with applause. The dachshund was pleased – he had proven that even short legs can accomplish great things.

47 In 1932, a brave dachshund named Hector pulled a boy from a frozen lake. Despite his small stature, he grabbed the child by his coat and pulled him to shore. Hector was celebrated and received a medal—and presumably a giant bone.

48 A dachshund in Australia was known for regularly playing with a kangaroo. The unlikely duo would bound together across meadows and fields. Tourists thought it was a show, but the two were simply best friends looking for adventure.

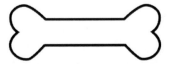

49 In the USA, a dachshund suddenly strayed from the track during a dog race and ran straight to a food stand. Instead of winning, he chose a sausage held by a spectator. The crowd laughed, and the dog was celebrated anyway.

50 A dachshund named "Gustav" from Sweden brought his owner shoes every day. The funny thing? He always brought his left shoe. Neither the right nor any other object seemed interesting. The owner has given up trying to understand the logic.

51 During a storm in England, a dachshund named "Bruno" saved his entire family. He barked incessantly until the sleeping residents left the house—just in time before a tree crashed onto the roof. A little hero with a big voice.

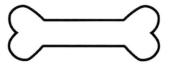

52 The dachshund "Sparky" from the USA once ran across a baseball diamond and stole the umpire's cap. Instead of catching him, the entire stadium laughed as the little troublemaker proudly made his rounds. A moment for the history books.

53 A dachshund in Germany found a bag containing 5,000 euros in cash and brought it to his owner. The owner was delighted and donated the money to an animal shelter as a thank you for his dog's honesty. The dachshund? He was given a huge steak to celebrate.

54 Every day, a dachshund who had befriended a canary sat in a small café in Paris. The bird often sat on his head while the dachshund remained still. The two became a local landmark, attracting daily visitors.

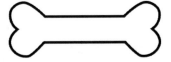

55 A British dachshund named "Milo" walked 15 kilometers home after falling out of a car. Despite the rain and cold, he made it across country roads and meadows to his front door. There, soaking wet but content, he waited for his family.

56 A dachshund from Japan became known for walking to the same bus stop every morning to see off his owner. He was there to pick him up promptly at 6 p.m. Loyalty can also have four paws and a long back.

57 In the USA, a dachshund won a talent contest by pretending to sleep "on command." His trick: He actually slept – every time. The audience loved him, and the dachshund seemed to enjoy the extra rest.

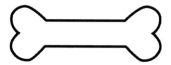

Dackel-Stories
Adventure in miniature

58 A German dachshund managed to collect 20 toys in his basket – and guard them all. No one was allowed to touch them, even if they were distributed. A true collector who protected his treasures like a pro.

59 A New York City dachshund took over Instagram by riding the subway daily while sitting in a designer bag. His relaxed demeanor and trademark "dachshund look" made him a viral star and a daily highlight for commuters.

60 A dachshund named "Loki" in Finland accidentally chased a reindeer. After five minutes, he realized the animal was too big and proudly returned. His owners called it "the quickest realization of his life."

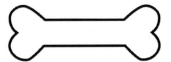

CHAPTER 5

Dachshund-German
What "woof" means

61 A drawn-out "woof" means: "I'm here, I'm awake, and something's wrong—or something cool is about to happen." The dachshund usually doesn't know what that means. But just to be on the safe side, the whole family is alerted.

62 A loud, rhythmic "woof-woof-woof" means: "Something's outside and I'm ready to report it." Whether it's the mailman, a gust of wind, or a beetle remains to be seen. But the dachshund will insist it was vital.

63 The deep, muffled "woof" with a growl undertone means: "I don't quite agree." This could be a new piece of furniture, an oversized vacuum cleaner, or the neighbor's cat. The dachshund is making it clear: "I'm monitoring the situation closely."

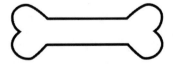

64 An excited, repeated "woof-woof-woof" with a wildly wagging tail means: "You're back! Where have you been? I haven't seen you in ages!" Whether you've been gone for an hour or just five minutes makes no difference to a dachshund.

65 The whining "woohoo," accompanied by a dachshund look, means: "My bowl is empty and that's not okay." This sound can sometimes be heard even when the bowl is full. A dachshund will always find a reason to complain about his food level.

66 A sudden, short "WOOF!" in the middle of sleep shows: "I'm dreaming! And something important!" Dachshunds are known for barking in their dreams, probably because they dream of exciting adventures or a never-ending sausage buffet.

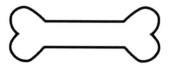

67 The energetic, short "woof-woof" when seeing a squirrel means: "Enemy spotted! I'm going to chase you!" Even if its legs are short and the squirrel has long since disappeared into the tree, the dachshund remains brave - at least in its imagination.

68 A monotonous, steady "woof-woof-woof" in front of the refrigerator door says very clearly: "I know what's in there and I need it now." A dachshund is a master at convincing everyone that he is about to starve to death.

69 A nasty growl-woof when a dachshund encounters something new means, "This is being checked out!" Whether it's a new box or a vacuum cleaner, he must critically inspect everything before it enters his territory. Distrust is part of the dachshund's strategy.

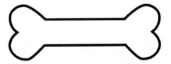

70 The high-pitched "woof-woof" in the garden, combined with hectic running, means: "I'm patrolling, everything is under control!" For the dachshund, the garden is a kingdom, and every ant or flower is checked for safety and barked at if necessary.

71 The sharp, excited "woof-woof-woof" when the doorbell rings means: "Alarm! A stranger or food delivery person is approaching!" The dachshund firmly believes that he must defend the house – until the visitor defuses the situation with snacks.

72 A quiet, offended "woof" when ignored means, "I'm disappointed in you." This often happens when the dachshund realizes that his request for a snack has been ignored. He will retreat with drooping ears to intensify his fuss.

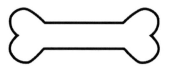

Dachshund-German
What "woof" means

73 A squealing "woof-woof-woooof" when the door is closed means, "Why can't I come in? I'm important!" A dachshund finds it unacceptable to be excluded from somewhere. After all, he might miss something crucial to his life.

74 A rhythmic "woof – pause – woof" directed at the neighbor's cat says: "Get off my lawn, you intruder!" The dachshund gives an impressive warning, even though he knows that he is usually too slow to chase after it.

75 The half-hearted "woof" when a ball is overlooked under the sofa says, "Get that out of the way. Now." A dachshund expects his human to solve his problems. It's not his job to search under furniture —after all, he has other things to do.

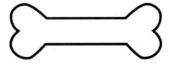

CHAPTER 6

Stubborn Studies
Dachshunds are always right

76 Dachshunds have excellent hearing, but will deliberately ignore you. If you call "Come here!" and the dachshund just tilts its head to the side, it means, "I heard you. I'm still thinking about it." A dachshund never follows commands that don't fit into its plan.

77 A dachshund decides for himself whether to sit or simply stay still. The trick behind this: Make him believe it's his idea. Praise, reward, bribe – dachshunds are master negotiators with a very clear sense of their own interests.

78 If a dachshund suddenly stops on a walk and doesn't take another step, it has discovered something important: either a particularly interesting trail or the perfect reason to be carried. The dachshund decides when to move on.

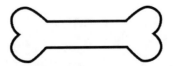

Stubborn Studies
Dachshunds are always right

79 Dachshunds like to test their humans. If they bark and you give in, they win. As soon as the bowl is full or the sofa is cleared, they know: "I'm the boss here." Give in once, and the dachshund takes over the entire daily planning.

80 A dachshund will always sit by the door if he wants to go out. If you don't react quickly enough, he'll look at you like an incompetent servant. The dachshund doesn't think you're the boss—more like his personal assistant, ready to run.

81 Dachshunds have an incredible talent for convincing themselves they're right. A chewed-up sofa? "I thought it was a toy." A stolen snack? "It was there for me." Guilt? None. The dachshund always has reasons.

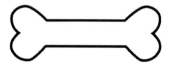

82 A dachshund won't let you pull on the leash. Instead, he'll get you to walk in his direction. The trick? A determined look, a firm stance, and the absolute conviction that he knows the best way.

83 The dachshund decides when it's playtime. It's time to get off work? Fine, but now it's time to play. He brings you a toy and sits in front of you until you give in. "Ignoring" is not an option for a dachshund - he always wins.

84 Dachshunds have a special way of saying "no": They sit down, stare at you, and don't move an inch. A "sit-down" in dachshund form. The idea behind it? "Your plan was bad, mine is better."

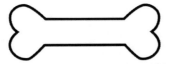

85 A dachshund never runs to the bowl when you fill it. He strolls leisurely and lets you know he doesn't need it. "Food? Yes, thank you. But please show a little more respect for the little ruler of the house."

86 If a dachshund wants to sit on the sofa and you say "no," he'll just stare at you until you give in. Dachshunds have an unparalleled talent for testing their owners' nerves—and always winning.

87 The dachshund will stay where he wants, for as long as he wants. A walk in the woods can become a test of patience if the dachshund decides he has to sniff out EVERYTHING in that one spot. Will he continue? Only if he allows it.

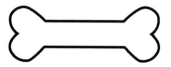

88 A dachshund will do anything to enforce its decisions. It will lie down in the middle of your desk chair, just when you're about to work. "My place. Your problem." A stubborn dog knows how to defend its comfort zone.

89 If a dachshund doesn't want something, you can forget it. A bath? "Never!" A new bed? "Why? My old one is perfect." Dachshunds won't accept any new things they haven't decided on themselves. Arguments are pointless.

90 A dachshund doesn't want to hear anything he doesn't want to hear. The word "vet" suddenly makes him go deaf. A dachshund is so good at selective hearing that you'll wonder if you even spoke.

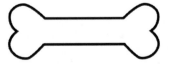

CHAPTER 7

Number magic
Statistics for furry friends

91 Dachshunds have an average of 42 teeth—perfect for crunchy snacks. The interesting thing? They also enjoy using them for playing, chewing, and shredding slippers. Their small jaws are surprisingly strong for such short legs and long bodies.

92 The record for the most puppies in a dachshund litter is 12! A dachshund mom miracle gave birth to this record-breaking litter. Imagine 12 little furry sausages scampering around at the same time.

93 Dackel gehören zu den Top 10 der beliebtesten Hunderassen weltweit. Ihre charmante Sturheit und ihr treuer Blick machen sie unwiderstehlich. Kein Wunder also, dass jährlich Millionen Dackel-Fotos in sozialen Medien die Herzen erobern.

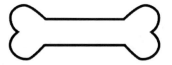

94 On average, a dachshund sleeps 12 to 14 hours a day. That's almost half its life. But beware, should the mailman arrive—the dachshund is wide awake within seconds and ready for loud action.

95 Dachshunds can live up to 20 years, making them one of the longest-living dog breeds. Statistically speaking, their stubbornness keeps them fit: They decide for themselves when they're tired and simply ignore anything that doesn't fit their schedule.

96 A fully grown standard dachshund has a body length of 45-50 cm—more than twice its height. Their shape is reminiscent of a sausage, but that doesn't bother them. Their motto? "Short dog, big presence."

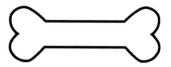

97 A dachshund can understand up to 100 different words and commands. Whether he responds to them is another matter, however. He knows exactly what "come here" means - but usually decides whether it's worth following.

98 The loudest dachshund bark ever recorded reached 115 decibels—as loud as a chainsaw. That's impressive for a dog barely knee-high. Postal carriers around the world can probably confirm this record.

99 A dachshund runs at an average speed of 10 km/h, but if he sees a squirrel, he can sometimes reach 15 km/h. His short legs give it their all. A marathon, however, isn't his goal—a snack at the finish line is more his goal.

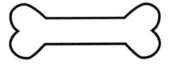

100 A dachshund's nose is 40 times more sensitive than a human's. It can even smell individual ingredients in food. Statistically, a dachshund sniffs about 100,000 times a day—especially if there's a smell of sausages.

101 A dachshund's paws can make 30 digging movements per minute. An unattended yard can quickly become a battlefield. For a dachshund, this means success all around.

102 On average, dachshunds bark two to three times more often than other dogs. This doesn't mean they're nervous—they just want everyone to hear them. Statistically, dachshunds are considered the best "house guards" among small breeds.

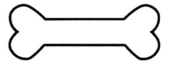

103 The smallest documented dachshund was only 12 cm tall and 18 cm long—a true miniature wonder. Despite his size, he was just as courageous as his larger counterparts and defended his territory with just as loud a voice.

104 The average walk with a dachshund takes 15 minutes longer because they want to sniff everywhere. A dachshund has no sense of time—only an insatiable curiosity that makes every flower, every puddle, and every blade of grass interesting.

105 Dachshunds have an amazing appetite: An 8 kg dog can eat up to 400 grams of food in one sitting. That's about 5% of its body weight – and it might still pretend to be hungry with its wide eyes.

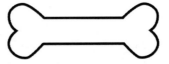

CHAPTER 8

Dachshund gags
Humor on short legs

106 The dachshund was probably designed by nature to test your patience. From ignoring commands to barking at midnight, he's convinced he's doing everything right. After all, he's not a dog—he's a personality.

107 Dachshunds have two speeds: "Look how fast I can run!" and "I'm not moving." Depending on his mood, he decides whether to chase the squirrel today or force you to carry him home.

108 A dachshund is like a toddler on four paws: always curious, usually stubborn, and with a knack for getting into trouble at the most inopportune times. An unattended sandwich is practically a lost cause.

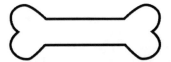

109 When a dachshund looks at you in the morning, it means, "It's time for breakfast." If you ignore him, he'll take it to the next level: quiet whining, paw nudges, and finally, a deliberate pounce on your belly. Good mood guaranteed.

110 A dachshund at the vet is like an actor at an Oscar ceremony. The look says, "How could you do this to me?" The drama only ends when the last biscuit has been fed and he is celebrated as a "survivor."

111 The dachshund has a natural instinct for sausages. If you try to hide one, he'll find it—whether it's in your pocket, under your pillow, or behind your back. A dachshund is more precise than a sniffer dog at an airport.

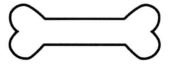

112 If a dachshund barks at the door and you open the wrong one, he'll look at you like an incompetent butler. "Wrong, man. I meant the refrigerator door." He has his priorities, and you should know them.

113 A dachshund in a puddle is a feat of physics. How it manages to stir up so much water with its short legs remains a mystery. The only solution after that? A dachshund bath, which, of course, it's not very cooperative.

114 The dachshund loves to lie in the sun. He can chill out like a pro for hours – and woe betide anyone who casts a shadow over his spot. His indignant look says, "I was here first. Move your big head away."

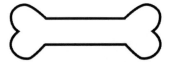

115 A dachshund never just looks at you—he sees through your soul. His gaze asks, "Why are you so slow at feeding?" Or, "Why are you sitting there while I need a ball?" The dachshund stare is pure manipulation in cute form.

116 Dachshunds are world champions at hiding toys. A ball that disappeared six months ago suddenly appears under the sofa – just as you're vacuuming. The dachshund will judge you for discovering its hiding place.

117 Why does the dachshund tilt his head when you talk to him? He's not doing it because he's listening. He's thinking, "How do I explain to this person that this isn't a sausage, but a vacuum cleaner?"

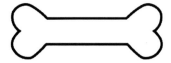

Dachshund gags
Humor on short legs

118 A dachshund in winter: "Cold? No thanks." If he notices that there's snow outside, he might just sit and wait. A dachshund decides for himself when the weather is acceptable—usually not until spring.

119 The dachshund hasn't made any mistakes —he's made "courageous decisions." Whether he knocks over a flowerpot or breaks your new shoe, his look tells you it was your fault, not his. "You should have hidden it!"

120 Dachshunds love snacks, but they're also gourmets. If you offer them dry food instead of sausage, they'll give you a critical look that says it all: "Excuse me, what is THAT? I thought we had a certain standard here."

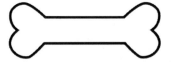

CHAPTER 9

Dachshund myths
Dog, Hero, Legend

Dachshund myths
Dog, Hero, Legend

121 The dachshund was once considered invulnerable, at least in its own mind. It's said that a dachshund once tried to confront a bear. The bear ran away— perhaps out of respect, perhaps because it didn't feel like arguing.

122 In ancient Germany, people believed that dachshunds could sniff out treasures buried deep in caves. They were allowed to crawl into caves, and when they barked, they eagerly began digging. The treasures? Mostly mice, but hope remained.

123 A myth says that dachshunds never get tired. In fact, they simply don't show it— until they fall asleep in the middle of the living room. Because being tired doesn't mean the dachshund is any less stubborn.

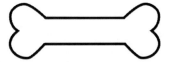

124 It was once thought that dachshunds could drive away ghosts with their barking. They were the perfect guards against invisible enemies. Whether the ghosts really left or were just protecting their ears remains a mystery to this day.

125 In England, there's the legend of the Dachshund Knight, a dog who saved a king's life by lighting a bonfire. How? The dog pulled burning wood toward him. Even if this is historically questionable, the story lives on.

126 It is said that in ancient times, a dachshund scared off a lion. The lion saw the little dog and was so confused that it decided to run away. Moral of the story: Even the king of beasts wouldn't mess with a dachshund.

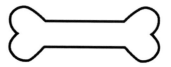

Dachshund myths
Dog, Hero, Legend

127 An old superstition says that dachshunds that shake their ears can predict rain. In fact, they also shake their ears when their bowl is empty or when they're tired of arguing.

128 In France, it's said that dachshunds were little witch hunters. They were supposed to track down witches and evil spirits hiding in badger sets. Who needs magic when you have a dachshund who scrutinizes everything?

129 A legend tells of a dachshund who "saved" an entire forest. A fire broke out, and the dog barked until the villagers arrived. The forest remained unharmed, and the little dachshund received an extra portion of sausage.

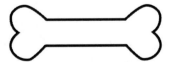

Dachshund myths
Dog, Hero, Legend

130 Some believe dachshunds have supernatural stamina. Apparently, a dachshund once ran after a horse for a whole day. Realistic? Perhaps. He'd certainly be stubborn enough to show he could keep up.

131 It's said that in the 18th century, a dachshund defended an entire castle by waking the guards with loud barking. The attackers fled in panic, believing an army had been alerted. In fact, it was just the dachshund.

132 A myth says that dachshunds love treasure and hide anything that glitters. Although they're not true pirates, they have a knack for "burying" socks, toys, and treats in the strangest corners.

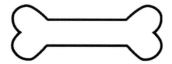

Dachshund myths
Dog, Hero, Legend

133 In Bavaria, dachshunds were believed to have the ability to drive away earth spirits. When a dachshund dug, it was trying to scare the spirits away. Today we know: it was looking for mice. So the spirits never had anything to fear.

134 An old superstition says that a dachshund is no one's friend unless he chooses to be. This legend is true: Anyone who gains a dachshund's trust will have a friend for life—but there are no shortcuts.

135 It's said that dachshunds can see straight into the soul. Their piercing gaze is said to read minds and uncover secrets. In fact, most of the time, they're just staring at that last slice of pizza you were secretly trying to eat.

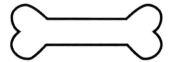

CHAPTER 10

Dachshund luxury
Beds and coats

Dachshund luxury
Beds and coats

136 A dachshund decides which bed is his—and it's definitely not the dog bed you bought. Instead, he prefers the sofa, your pillow, or freshly washed laundry. Luxury means sleeping exactly where you didn't plan.

137 Dachshunds love coats, but only for practical reasons. A wet or cold dachshund is an unhappy dachshund. So he wears the coat like a designer suit—and expects all the neighbors to comment on how good he looks.

138 Dachshunds have a special sense for cozy places. A dog bed? Nice. But they'll find the warmest blanket in the house and make it their own. Even if you're lying underneath it, the dachshund decides how much space you have left.

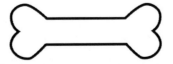

Dachshund luxury
Beds and coats

139 A luxurious dachshund coat isn't an accessory, it's a statement. A dachshund in a checked tweed coat says, "I'm small, but very important." And woe betide anyone who doubts that—the outraged stare comes free of charge.

140 Dachshunds prefer blankets with multiple layers. A bed with just one layer isn't enough. The higher the blanket pile, the better. For them, this means comfort—for you, it's a puzzle, since the dachshund sleeps in the middle of a pile of laundry.

141 A dachshund wearing a tailored coat walks like a king. You can practically hear him thinking, "Look at me! I'm the star of this place." He skillfully ignores the laughter of the other dogs in the park.

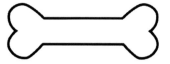

142 Luxury is non-negotiable for a dachshund. A dog pillow from a discount store? "Unbearable!" A memory foam bed that supports his long back? "Finally, a human who understands me."

143 A dachshund knows the value of a cozy nap. His bed needs to be soft, warm, and strategically placed—preferably close to a radiator or in the sun. You can offer it on the floor, but he still prefers the sofa.

144 Dachshunds prefer furniture that's appropriate for their height. If the bed is too high, they'll look at you as if to say, "Help me or carry me." At the same time, they expect the climb to look majestic—and that only works with your support.

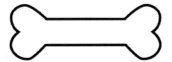

Dachshund luxury
Beds and coats

145 A cold dachshund will let you know he's unhappy. The shivering isn't accidental—it's a tactic. A cozy sweater or a chic coat will solve the problem. Luxurious warmth is, after all, a basic right.

146 Dachshunds love pillows, and the bigger the better. A small pillow? "Funny." A giant pillow that blocks the sofa? "Yes, exactly that!" The dachshund manages to take possession of a pillow so you don't even try to get it back.

147 A luxurious dachshund has high standards. A velvet or faux fur bed is his idea of comfort. If it bears his name, he'll sit proudly on it like a king—at least until he discovers your bed is "even better."

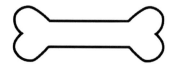

148 Dachshunds are masters of adaptation: If the weather is bad and they don't have a coat, they'll look at you accusingly. They want you to know: "Just going out like that? In the rain? What do you think I am —a Labrador?"

149 The dachshund doesn't just sleep in his bed—he arranges it. Pillows are scratched, blankets are rolled up, and only when everything is perfect does he settle down contentedly. After all, luxury requires proper preparation.

150 A dachshund doesn't need a castle to feel like royalty. A soft bed, a warm coat, and a bowl of the finest food are all he needs. But his expression says, "I deserve even more—where's my golden bowl?"

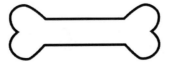

CHAPTER 11

Food facts
All about dachshund snacks.

Food facts
All about dachshund snacks.

151 Dachshunds don't just eat, they inhale. An 8-pound dachshund can devour a full meal in less than 30 seconds—and then, with a sad expression, act as if he hadn't eaten anything for days. A masterpiece of theatrical manipulation.

152 Dachshunds are snack specialists. The mere crunch of a bag of chips is enough to jolt them from a deep sleep. Their hearing is so precise that they can even distinguish whether you're unwrapping vegetables or sausage—the latter, they'll be there in a flash.

153 A dachshund can stare into its owner's eyes for 20 minutes straight while eating. That look says it all: "Sharing is fair. You have two halves, I'll take one. Actually, I could take both if that's easier."

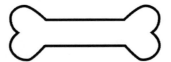

Food facts
All about dachshund snacks.

154 The concept of "portioning" is foreign to dachshunds. Dachshunds can eat astonishing amounts. The problem? Their stomachs may be stretchy, but their bodies aren't. A study found that dachshunds are among the dogs most likely to struggle with weight problems.

155 Dachshunds love to hide snacks for later, in case hunger strikes. Under the sofa, behind the pillow, or in your shoe—he has a hiding place. The best part? He forgets half of it and proudly finds it weeks later.

156 A dachshund is convinced that anything that lands on the floor belongs to him. Whether it's a crumb, a whole sausage, or a broccoli floret, he'll sprint faster than Usain Bolt to secure it. Dachshund rule number 1: Everything edible belongs to him by law.

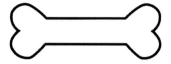

Food facts
All about dachshund snacks.

157 When a dachshund gets a treat, it's not just food—it's an event. He carefully picks it up, walks into another room, puts it down, sniffs it again, and looks at you: "Any more?" For him, snacks are like little rituals.

158 A dachshund can detect a full refrigerator with his super nose even through closed doors. If you open it, he stands behind you like a shadow, watching your every move. "For me? No? Okay, I'll stay here and watch anyway."

159 It's said that dachshunds have a "treat memory." If you show them where the snacks are once, they'll never forget where to find them. A dachshund can even identify sounds like the opening of a specific kitchen cabinet.

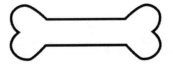

160 A dachshund can't lie, but he can cheat. If he eats a treat, he'll go to another family member and pretend he hasn't had one yet. Dachshunds aren't just smart— they know how to win hearts (and snacks).

161 Dachshunds love everything that's forbidden. Chocolate, cake, or pizza? That's exactly what they want. An unattended table is a buffet. A dachshund doesn't let his size stop him – he climbs, jumps, and pushes his way forward.

162 A dachshund doesn't just chew—he savors. A pig's ear or a bone can keep him busy for hours. He looks so content that you wonder if he just had a three-course Michelin-starred meal.

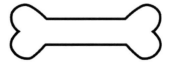

163 Dachshunds have a special technique when it comes to snacks: They take a treat, carry it to a "secret spot," and eat it there. The reason? I don't know. They're probably afraid you'll take it away from them otherwise.

164 A dachshund immediately recognizes when you're cheating at food. A small bite from the table? He saw it. His gaze practically pierces you, saying, "You ate that without giving me any. Do you really think I didn't notice?"

165 For a dachshund, dinner isn't the end of the day, but rather the starting signal for a "snack marathon." As soon as his bowl is empty, the mission begins: "I'll find something else." Whether crumbs or leftovers, the dachshund leaves no stone unturned.

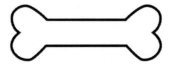

CHAPTER 12

Dachshund tricks
Who is educating whom here?

Dachshund tricks
Who is educating whom here?

166 A dachshund never learns "sit"—he teaches you to accept "wait." He looks at you, considers, and decides whether it's worth it. If he then sits, it seems so patronizing that you reward him with pride—just as he planned.

167 A dachshund doesn't perform tricks—it interprets commands. "Down" might mean: I'll curl up comfortably on your sofa. A dachshund decides for itself how many tricks it will perform today for a treat.

168 You think you're teaching your dachshund "stay"? He's actually teaching you how long you can stand and wait. When he runs off on "stay," he's testing whether you'll chase him—and most of the time, you won't win the game.

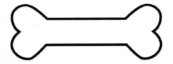

Dachshund tricks
Who is educating whom here?

169 Dachshunds can open doors – not physically, but with their charm. If he sits in front of the door and stares at you with wide eyes, you've given up within five seconds. So who was training whom here? That's right: the dachshund, you.

170 The dachshund trains you to applaud every time he does something. If he jumps onto the sofa, you look impressed. If he brings you a ball, you praise him profusely. He knows that praise is the best way to keep you entertained.

171 A dachshund knows exactly how to avoid "give paw." When you ask him to, he'll turn around, yawn, or suddenly scratch his ear. The message? "I'm busy. Ask me later." But as soon as snacks appear, he'll master the trick perfectly.

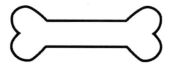

Dachshund tricks
Who is educating whom here?

172 Dachshunds don't misunderstand "fetch the stick"—they understand it too well. They fetch it, but put it down three meters away. Why? Because they know you'll go there to throw it again anyway. A dachshund never plays without winning.

173 The dachshund will stare at you until you give up and go for treats. This is called mental control. You thought you were training him with snacks? In fact, he's training you to constantly run to the kitchen.

174 Want to teach your dachshund not to climb onto the table? He'll see it as a challenge. He'll wait until you're not looking and sit triumphantly in the middle. A dachshund never fails—he just tries new tactics.

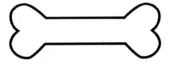

175 A dachshund ignores the word "no" perfectly. Instead of reacting, he looks at you, blinks, and yawns demonstratively. He wants you to know: Your "no" has no power. The only thing that motivates him is snacks or toys.

176 The Dachshund has a talent for "leave me alone" training. If you ask him to play and he just stays down, you'll quickly learn that it's his time, not yours. This is how the Dachshund shows you who's really in charge.

177 You think your dachshund has learned to fetch the ball? No, he's taught you to throw it. He decides when he's had enough and simply leaves the ball. The game only ends when the dachshund thinks it's right.

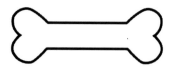

178 A dachshund doesn't need to be called back. He hears you, he sees you—and he still doesn't come. Why? Because he knows you'll come to him anyway. Patience is the real training for dachshund owners, not for the dog.

179 Dachshunds train you to always share. At every meal, they sit in front of you and stare at you until you give in. The result? You eat less, the dachshund eats more – and they've performed their "trick" perfectly.

180 A dachshund teaches you that furniture is only optional for humans. Your chair, sofa, or bed belongs to him. He trains you to look for alternatives while he claims the best spots.

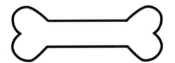

CHAPTER 13

Sniffing professionals
Nose always on the ground

181 A dachshund's nose has 220 million olfactory cells—compared to your measly 5 million. This means that while you see a garden, a dachshund sees an entire universe of smells. And he has to examine each one immediately.

182 A dachshund can smell a snack from 50 meters away. Think you've hidden your sausage well? The dachshund has known where it is for a long time - he's just waiting for you to give in and hand it over. Hiding it is pointless.

183 The term "sniffing" describes a philosophy of life for dachshunds. Every blade of grass, every leaf, and every speck of dust has a story. For dachshunds, the world is a book of smells, and they read every page—no matter how long it takes.

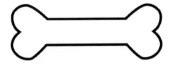

184 A dachshund's nose can distinguish between smells that are days old. This means that a crumb of pizza that fell under the sofa last week is just as exciting to him as a freshly made plate. A miniature detective.

185 Sniffing is a full-time activity for dachshunds. You want to go for a jog? He wants to sniff. You want to walk further? He wants to check again what the ant colony experienced last night. Dachshund time simply moves at a slower pace.

186 A dachshund sniffs about 300 times per minute when outside. This means that while you're taking a leisurely step, the dachshund has already scanned the entire area. Multitasking is his specialty.

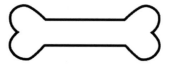

187 A dachshund never simply raises its nose to sniff the air. When it does, it means, "I know something you don't." Most of the time, it's already on a squirrel, a cat, or the smell of your breakfast.

188 The dachshund's nose is not only efficient, but also selectively honest. The smell of food? Immediately exciting. Your sweaty socks? Repulsive. When the dachshund turns away, you know it's time for the washing machine.

189 A dachshund doesn't sniff around aimlessly. He works like a professional detective: picking up a trail, finding a target, and securing his prey. The problem? The "prey" is often just a stone or a leaf that, for some reason, seems suspicious to him.

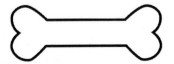

190 A dachshund doesn't feel guilty if he finds something edible while sniffing. An unattended sausage in the park? For him, it's a gift from the universe. Sniffing turns him into the Indiana Jones of the dog world.

191 As soon as a dachshund starts moving his nose, he forgets the world around him. Calling, luring, shaking treats – nothing works. The dachshund is in another dimension where only smells matter.

192 They say a dachshund's nose is never wrong. If he sniffs your backpack, he knows you're carrying snacks. You can deny it all you want—he'll keep nagging you until you give in and share.

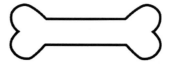

193 A dachshund can sniff so intensely on a walk that after 10 minutes, you haven't even covered 100 meters. While you're annoyed, the dachshund is happy: He's already created an entire olfactory encyclopedia of the park.

194 The dachshund uses its nose not only for searching for food, but also for social analysis. A strange dog has been here? It knows. What did the dog eat yesterday? That too. The dachshund's nose is a high-performance scanner with a built-in archive.

195 A dachshund never just raises its head—it's a statement. If it suddenly raises its nose in the air and sniffs, it means, "Attention, something exciting is happening." What that is? Only the dachshund knows.

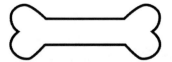

CHAPTER 14

Friend vs. Foe
Cat terror included

196 For a dachshund, the neighbor's cat is both enemy number one and the world's most fascinating mystery. He barks at it, chases it, and then asks himself, "Why does she just ignore me? I'm the boss here!" The cat knows better.

197 A dachshund and a vacuum cleaner - the duel of the century. As soon as the vacuum cleaner starts up, the dachshund becomes a brave warrior. With his fur bristling and a bark of protest, he makes it clear: "I won't let this roaring monster drive me away!"

198 For dachshunds, mail carriers are like supervillains. Every day, the same person shows up and dares to come to the house. It's clear to the dachshund: An opponent who returns regularly needs consistent resistance—by barking, of course.

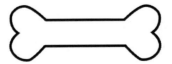

Friend vs. Foe
Cat terror included

199 The dachshund believes he can catch squirrels. Every time. No matter how many failures he experiences, his hope remains unshakable. The squirrel, however, stays cool and thinks to himself: "That little wobbly hunter again – good luck next time!"

200 A dachshund can watch a bird in the garden for hours while barking. For the dachshund, the bird is a provocateur who breaks the rules: "I'm not allowed to fly, so you shouldn't be allowed to either!" Logic that only dachshunds understand.

201 The mirror is a young dachshund's greatest enemy. "Who is this dog that's mimicking me?" After a while, he begins to ignore his opponent – and considers himself the winner. Ultimately, the mirror never gives up, but neither does the dachshund.

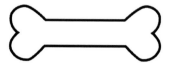

202 A dachshund fighting a mop is a real thriller. The mop moves, the dachshund reacts. A dance of attack and defense, in which the dog always emerges as the moral victor. The mop, after all, has no heart and no courage.

203 A dachshund bravely faces anything bigger than him—even cows or horses. In his world, it's not size that counts, but courage. The horse may look confused, but the dachshund walks away proudly: "Another giant chased away!"

204 The dachshund regularly "trains" the neighbor's dog. No matter how big the other dog is, the dachshund makes it clear: "This is my territory." A clarifying bark, an imposing gait—and everyone knows who's the real boss.

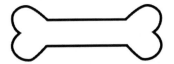

205 A dachshund handles mice with the utmost professionalism. They are his declared rivals in the garden. A molehill? Another reason to dig deep. His mission is clear: every intruder will be hunted down —or at least barked at.

206 The house cat is in charge, but the dachshund doesn't give up. He nudges her, provokes her, and when she ignores him, he barks in offense. But if she hits him, he flees to the sofa, thinking, "I was just asking, why so aggressive?"

207 A dachshund and a broom are eternal enemies. As soon as it enters the room, the fight begins. The dachshund grabs the bristles and does everything he can to stop the thing. For him, it's clear: "I'll protect the house from this intrusive opponent!"

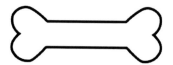

208 Flies are a real nuisance for dachshunds. They're small, fast, and always escape at the last moment. The chase is a drama in which the dachshund is certain: "This one time, I'll catch them." A perpetual dream.

209 A dachshund considers feather dusters to be rebellious creatures. As soon as he sees them, he begins his mission: stop the duster and save the house. He skillfully ignores the fact that the duster is just a cleaning tool—he sees it as a worthy opponent.

210 The dachshund knows no fear when it comes to balloons. He barks, snaps, and tries to defeat them - until they burst. Then he turns around, takes a quick sniff, and acts as if he never had anything to do with them. The winner remains unfazed.

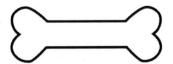

CHAPTER 15

Dachshund vs. Dog
Dog breeds in comparison

Dachshund vs. Dog
Dog breeds in comparison

211 The dachshund may be small, but its ego is huge. While a Labrador waits for your praise, a dachshund praises itself: "Of course I did well. What did you think?" Other dogs work for recognition; dachshunds expect it.

212 A Golden Retriever happily retrieves balls, while the Dachshund thinks, "Why are you taking that thing away if you want it back? Go find it yourself." A Dachshund only retrieves when it's in his dignity—or when snacks are involved.

213 A Border Collie learns 100 commands and carries them out. The Dachshund knows all of them but deliberately ignores them. His look says, "I know exactly what you want, but my time is more valuable than that. Call me back later."

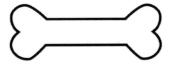

214 A Chihuahua barks to feel big. A dachshund barks because it believes it's already big. For it, every noise is a potential challenge to its authority—and its barking lets every neighbor know who's in charge.

215 The Dachshund and the German Shepherd both have guarding instincts. The difference? The German Shepherd will stand between you and danger. The Dachshund will boldly stand in front of it and bark so loudly that everyone thinks it's twice your size.

216 A pug snores while sleeping, a dachshund snores to demonstrate how comfortable it is. While the pug only grunts quietly, the dachshund sounds like a puffing steam locomotive. He enjoys his sleep – and lets everyone hear it.

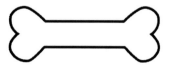

217 A poodle is getting a grooming and feels comfortable. A dachshund that needs a bath is like a miniature natural disaster. The look, the whining, the flight – a dachshund lets you know: "Water? For princes like me? Never."

218 A husky will run for miles through snow and cold. A dachshund, on the other hand, stays by the door when it's drizzling outside: "I'm not made for this weather. Bring me inside and lay down a blanket." A dachshund chooses luxury over adventure.

219 A beagle will follow its nose for hours through the forest. A dachshund will follow its nose too—only until the next snack or molehill. Afterward, it will look at you as if it had found the meaning of life, and you're interrupting its progress.

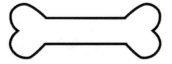

Dachshund vs. Dog
Dog breeds in comparison

220 A Dalmatian is elegant and athletic. A Dachshund, on the other hand, is the embodiment of "comfort meets stubbornness." While other dogs sprint, the Dachshund makes it clear: "My pace? Slow but steady." And he still wins.

221 A greyhound runs like lightning. A dachshund? It only runs fast when food is involved. And while the greyhound is admired for its elegance, the dachshund looks like a rolling sausage ball—and proudly so.

222 The Labrador loves water and jumps into the lake enthusiastically. The Dachshund stops at the water's edge, looks skeptical, and thinks, "Why would I do that? My fur is too precious for such a mess." Dachshunds and water are rarely friends.

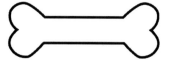

223 A Jack Russell Terrier runs around like a rubber ball. The dachshund watches and thinks, "Why waste so much energy? A nap on the couch is much more productive." The dachshund lives by the motto: "Smart, not hectic."

224 A St. Bernard brings barrels full of rescue supplies for avalanche victims. The dachshund brings only the bare essentials —himself and perhaps a treat he ate beforehand. His motto: "I'll rescue you as soon as I'm rested."

225 An Australian Shepherd enjoys working on commands and tasks. The Dachshund sets the tasks himself: "You pick up the leash, you open the door, and you give snacks. I'm the project manager here." The division of roles is clear.

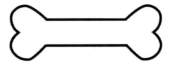

CHAPTER 16

Dachshund curiosities
Facts on short legs

Dachshund curiosities
Facts on short legs

226 A dachshund believes you're not its owner, but its personal assistant. Whether serving food, opening doors, or fetching toys—you have tasks to perform. A dachshund trains its owner with patience and a loyal gaze.

227 You want to work? The dachshund decides it's cuddle time. He sits down in front of your laptop, puts his paw on the keyboard, and says, "Priorities, human! I'm more important here than any email nonsense."

228 A dachshund expects its owner to understand all of its needs telepathically. If you guess wrong—for example, offering food instead of a walk—you'll get that inimitable look: "Wrong answer. Try again."

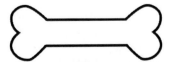

Dachshund curiosities
Facts on short legs

229 A dachshund will fool you into thinking you're "going for a walk together." In reality, he's taking you for a walk. He decides where to go, how long to sniff, and when to head back home. You're just the chauffeur at the other end of the leash.

230 Your dachshund has his own schedule. Breakfast? 7 a.m. sharp. Dinner? Punctual as the train. Delays are not tolerated. If you're not performing, he'll loudly remind you that he never forgets a snack.

231 A dachshund will teach you that beds aren't just for humans. If you roll over to make room, he'll already have taken over the center. The owner becomes a marginal dweller while the dachshund enjoys the kingdom.

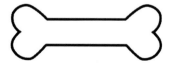

Dachshund curiosities
Facts on short legs

232 If your dachshund breaks something, he's showing you that you're wrong. A broken shoe? "You didn't clean it up." A chewed-up chair? "I needed something to do." The question of blame is always settled: It's the owner's fault.

233 The dachshund decides when playtime is over. If you bring the ball back and say, "Let's go!" he looks at you, sits down, and signals, "Enough for today. You can take a break now." His word is law.

234 A dachshund sees the sofa as a shared space—on his own terms. If you sit down, he lands on your lap. If you stand up, he curls up right in the middle. Your attempt to shoo him away is met with indignation and offended looks.

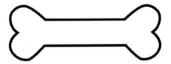

235 A dachshund makes you do things you never wanted to do. Like crawling on your knees to retrieve a lost toy from under the sofa. You're sure, "I'm training the dog." The dachshund thinks, "Good person. Well trained."

236 Are you trying to teach your dachshund not to jump on the table? He listens, nods inwardly—but does it anyway. You only have the illusion of control. He makes you feel like you're the boss, even though he's already won.

237 A dachshund has the ability to emotionally destroy its owner. You scold him, and he looks at you—ears drooping, head bowed, and the gaze of an innocent angel. In your head, you hear: "Was that really necessary?"

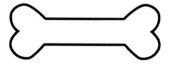

Dachshund curiosities
Facts on short legs

238 Dachshunds have no patience for bad moods. If you're sad or in a bad mood, he'll come over, sit in front of you, and stare: "Stop that. That won't get me any treats." Suddenly you laugh—and he wins.

239 If you don't share your food, the dachshund becomes a silent reproach. He stares at you until you give in. His look says, "You wanted to eat that by yourself? How selfish! Think of me and my poor, empty tummy."

240 Did you think the bed was too small for two? A dachshund will show you that he needs just enough space for himself - diagonally. While you lie uncomfortably, he snores peacefully. The dachshund has his priorities straight.

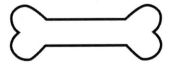

CHAPTER 17

And the master?
Dog leashes and can openers

241 The dachshund was originally bred in Germany to drive badgers out of their burrows. Its name comes from the German word "Dachs." Today, it has traded the forests for sofas, transforming from a brave hunting dog into the king of the couch.

242 Its long body and short legs made the dachshund perfect for underground hunting. But while it once explored badger sets, it now prefers warm blankets and cozy spots—the life of a couch potato is simply more appealing.

243 In the 16th century, dachshunds became known as brave hunting dogs, capable of tracking badgers even in tight burrows. Today, they prefer to hunt for treats or the best spot on the sofa—a significant but entirely successful change.

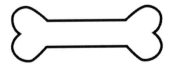

244 Dachshunds were bred for hunting in different sizes to suit different animals. From the standard dachshund to the miniature dachshund, they were true hunting experts. Today, size only matters when it comes to cuddling.

245 The dachshund's short legs were deliberately bred to allow him to crawl effortlessly into animal burrows. Today, he prefers to use those legs to march slowly but decisively to the refrigerator—especially when he smells snacks.

246 Dachshunds were once popular with hunters because they were not only brave but also incredibly resilient. This resilience is evident today in their ability to snooze for hours in their favorite spot—in style, of course.

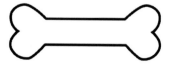

247 In the Middle Ages, dachshunds were considered heroes underground. They fought badgers and other animals. Today, they only fight against vacuum cleaners and their master's rules when they think they don't make sense.

248 Dachshunds were bred for various types of hunting. Rabbit-hunting dachshunds were experts at finding small burrows, while the larger dachshunds could also track wild boar. Today, their favorite missions are more leisurely in nature.

249 The breed became known for its tenacity and courage, even when facing larger animals. These qualities make them truly outstanding personalities to this day—both on the hunt and in everyday life with their owners.

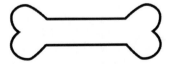

And the master?
Dog leashes and can openers

250 The dachshund has changed little over the centuries. Its strong body, short legs, and long back remain trademarks to this day. Only its habitat has changed: from the wilderness directly to the sofa.

251 The dachshund's long ears help guide scents to its nose—an advantage when hunting. Today, however, they're primarily used to look cute while the dachshund sits on the couch, wrapping its humans around its little finger.

252 Dachshunds weren't just meant for badgers—they could also track foxes and wild boars. Their versatility made them popular with hunters. Today, they're just as versatile: as playmates, cuddle buddies, and little rascals.

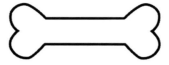

253 A standard dachshund could once chase badgers from burrows up to three meters deep. Today, he prefers to use his energy sniffing for snacks or climbing onto the sofa. Priorities change.

254 Dachshunds were once considered "guardians of the earth" for their ability to dig deep and track animals. Today, they guard their favorite spots in the house with just as much zeal—especially when it comes to the sofa.

255 In the 19th century, dachshunds were a symbol of strength and courage. Today, they symbolize humor and friendliness— but they have never lost their strong character. A true dachshund always retains a personality.

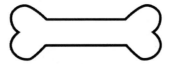

CHAPTER 18

Dachshund mishaps
Embarrassing on four paws

256 A dachshund tries to jump onto the sofa but gets stuck on the edge. Instead of being embarrassed, he looks at you as if it's all part of his plan. Of course, you carry him up—after all, the sofa is his rightful throne.

257 A dachshund chases a ball with great vigor - only to then run past it. The ball stays put, but the dachshund looks around searchingly, as if facing an invisible enemy. For him, this isn't a mistake, but rather "creative play."

258 A dachshund sticks its nose into a mouse hole and gets its ears stuck. Instead of trying to free itself, it starts barking— not out of panic, but to tell you: "I have a problem here, solve it now, human!"

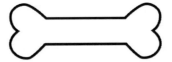

259 A dachshund slips on a freshly mopped floor, tries to catch himself, and ends up in a spectacular roll. Then he gets up, shakes himself, and acts as if nothing happened. A true pro when it comes to dignity.

260 A dachshund enthusiastically jumps into a puddle, only to discover he's getting wet. He limps back with an offended look, as if someone had tricked him. It's clear to him: The blame lies with you, not his own curiosity.

261 A dachshund chases a squirrel and gets stuck in a hedge. While you try to pull him out, he looks at you like a hero in a tight spot. The hedge? An overpowering opponent, but the dachshund will defeat him – with your help.

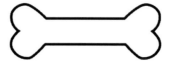

Dachshund mishaps
Embarrassing on four paws

262 A dachshund tries to scratch himself, but his short legs can't reach the right spot. He looks at you as if it's your fault and expects you to immediately step in as his "scratching assistant." Embarrassing? Only for you, not for him.

263 A dachshund steals a piece of bread from the table, runs away triumphantly—and trips over a rug. The bread flies in a high arc, but the dachshund acts as if it were all a planned stunt. The rug is given a reproachful look.

264 A dachshund enthusiastically digs a hole in the garden and gets his head stuck. He doesn't bark in panic—he barks like a boss giving orders: "Get me out of here, now!" For him, this is a team effort.

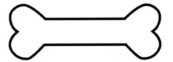

265 A dachshund confidently approaches a large dog, but stops when the dog barks back. He turns around, as if suddenly he has more important things to do, and gestures: "I didn't run away. I just didn't have time for this."

266 A dachshund sticks his head into an empty chip bag to grab the last crumbs and gets stuck. He runs blindly around the room, barking and stumbling. When you rescue him, he looks at you as if it's all your fault.

267 A dachshund tries to jump over a high curb, gets stuck, and falls back. He sits down, looks around, and signals, "I didn't want to go over anyway. It was just a test." His ego remains unshaken.

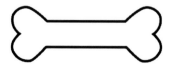

268 A dachshund energetically chases a bird that suddenly flies away. The dachshund stops, looks up at the sky, and growls as if the bird had betrayed him. "Fly? Unfair! Come down and fight like a real opponent!"

269 A dachshund sniffs a flower but is stung by a bee. He backs away, looks at the flower like a traitor, and decides that from now on, flowers are enemies. Sniffing? Only with caution and long thought.

270 A dachshund jumps into the car but gets stuck halfway up, waiting for you to push him. If you help, he acts like he let you do it to make you feel needed. "I could have done it myself, but okay."

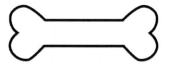

Thank you
for purchasing our book!

We hope you had a lot of fun with our crazy and funny facts.

If you enjoyed the book, we would be delighted if you would leave us a review on Amazon! Your feedback will help other customers make better purchasing decisions.

Share your opinion with us – and help us make even more people laugh!

Your Ben